Common Pronunciation Difficulties Observed Among Native Arabic Speakers Learning to Speak English

Common Pronunciation Difficulties Observed Among Native Arabic Speakers Learning to Speak English

JAMIL ABDULHADI

Will-EXCEL TESOL Institute

Rev. date: 07/10/2015

To order additional copies of this book, contact:
Xlibris
1-800-455-039
www.Xlibris.com.au
Orders@Xlibris.com.au
711355

CONTENTS

LIST OF TABLES

ACKNOWLEDGEMENT

I would like to take this chance to thank my wife and my daughter for the support they provided and their belief in me, as well as guidance they provided, without which I would have never been able to do this research.

DECLARATION

I, Jamil AbdulHadi, would like to declare that the contents included in this thesis stand for my individual work and have not been submitted for any examinations, academically as well as professionally, on any level previously. It also represents my very own views and is not essentially associated with the Will-EXCEL TESOL Institute.

ABSTRACT

Good English communication depends on correct grammar and vocabulary as well as proper pronunciation. Clear pronunciation is important for effective communication of the language.

There are various factors that contribute to the proper pronunciation of the words. The correct sound of the word can be learnt through phonics. Volume and pitch are also important factors. The loudness and tone of the language contribute to its meaning. Good pronunciation is not only learned through hearing the words of the language but is also acquired through speaking practice.

English is the third most spoken language in the world and the primary language of international businesses and academia. Hence, it is important for non-native people to learn the language as a tool for communication and knowledge assimilation.

There are various methodologies that can be adopted to learn English pronunciation. Arabic and English are two very different languages in terms of their writing system and direction of writing.

This is a major reason native Arabic speakers find it difficult to learn to speak English. The Arabic alphabet is different from the English alphabet. English pronunciation rules are considered arbitrary and inconsistent. Despite the discrepancies, English pronunciation is not without some general rules, and there are various rules for assisting in the correct pronunciation of the English language. There are also various systems for writing phonetic transcriptions of English words. Amongst these, the International Phonetic Alphabet (IPA) is the most popular system. There is also an alternative transcription system made. The system is known as the ASCII Phonetic Alphabet.

This research relied on both primary and secondary data. It developed two questionnaires related to phonological difficulties and the correct pronunciation. It also collected secondary data. All this data was analyzed, and findings and recommendations for the study were formulated.

CHAPTER 1

Introduction

Good English communication depends on correct grammar and vocabulary as well as proper pronunciation. Clear pronunciation is important for effective communication of the language. Phonics is a method of teaching English to beginners. In this method, each speech sound is represented with a single symbol. They are represented in a way that closely resembles how they actually sound. For the people who are not native speakers of the English language, learning phonics can assist in achieving a near-native accent of English language (Saylor 2012, p. n.d).

Different dialects of the English language vary in pronunciation. Some English speakers elongate vowels while speaking. Some English speakers have a nasal pronunciation to many words. These include New York state residents and Midwestern US residents. African Americans cut words short in phrases. Other speakers do not distinguish between vowel sounds. Hence *this* is pronounced the same as the word *these*. There are both positive and negative effects of poor pronunciation. Poor pronunciation gives the impression of the speaker being less literate or less intelligent. A person may lose a pay raise or a promotion because of not communicating well in English. Then again, distinct accents may also prove advantageous to people. A French restaurant may prefer waiters who speak English with a French accent. Certain movie roles have the requirement to simulate the real picture of the character. Hence a person speaking English in his own accent may be preferred (Saylor 2012, p. n.d).

There are various factors that contribute to the proper pronunciation of words. The correct sound of a word can be learnt through phonics. Volume and pitch are also important factors. The loudness and tone of the message contribute to its meaning. Good pronunciation is not only learned but also acquired through hearing the words of the language (Saylor 2012, p. n.d).

1.1 Background

English is the third most spoken language in the world. Mandarin Chinese ranks first in the list, and Spanish is the second most spoken language in the world. The approximate number of native speakers of the English language is 335 million. The following is a list of native speakers of some of the most widely spoken languages in the world.

Table 1: Most widely spoken languages in the world

Serial #	Language	Approximate number of speakers (in millions)
1	Chinese (Mandarin)	848
2	Spanish	406
3	English	335
4	Hindi	260
5	Arabic	223
6	Portuguese	202
7	Bengali	193
8	Russian	162
9	Japanese	122
10	Javanese	84.3

Source: *Ethnologue*, 2013.

English is a language spoken worldwide. Hence, it is important for non-native speakers to learn the language as a tool for communication and knowledge assimilation. Pronunciation can become very difficult for foreigners trying to learn the English language. English is not an especially phonetic language. A word may be spelled out in one way and said in another way. Hence, it is important to learn the pronunciation by practicing and listening to English phrases. It is important that students of English language are patient and diligent in their efforts.

There are various methodologies that can be adopted to learn English pronunciation. An English tutor who can converse with the person and correct his mispronunciation might be helpful. Another method is to use a phonetic alphabet chart to learn the sounds of English letters. Another approach can be to watch pronunciation videos. One more way of correcting pronunciation is to join a club or seek help of an English-speaking friend. Talking daily to such a person helps in correcting mistakes in pronunciation (Perez 2013, p. n.d). Reading loudly from books and magazines also helps in English pronunciation improvement. English teaching discs and programs have large sections of text that can be listened to for improving pronunciation (Buleen 2013, p. n.d).

English pronunciation activities can also prove useful in improving the pronunciation of non-native speakers. There are words in English that sound similar. For example, *man* and *men* or *three* and *free*. An instructor may conduct an activity in the class.

He may call two students. He can then write two words on the board that sound similar. These two words are written on each side of a flash card. Then the instructor shows Student A one side of the flash card and asks him to read the word aloud. Student B circles the word on the board that he hears. It identifies whether Student B circles the same word that was shown to Student A on the flash card. Another activity might be to arrange students in a circle. The instructor then writes a sentence on a paper and shows it to the first student. That student whispers the sentence to the next student, who then whispers it to the next student. The last student says the sentence in a loud voice. This sentence may be compared with the one written on the paper.

Regular verbs, where their past tense ends in *ed*, are difficult to differentiate in pronunciation. An instructor can write the word *Now* on one end of the board and the word *Before* on the other end of the board. Now the instructor calls the students one by one. He hands him a paper with a sentence that uses a regular verb. If a student hears the present tense, he stands under Now. If a student hears the past tense, he stands under Before. This will enable students to differentiate among different forms of verbs (Page 2013, p. n.d).

1.2 Statement of the Problem

Learning the English language is important for effective communication as English is widely used in the world of business and for official correspondence. There is also a huge body of academic work and research available in the English language. Those people who do not have English as their native language try to learn English through various learning methods and sources. Their regional background and accent affect their learning curve as people of different regions face different problems and issues related to the learning of the English language. In this context, Arabic speakers face problems and difficulties in learning English at both phonetic and phonological levels. The English pronunciation guides /booklets / introductory notes in bilingual (English to Arabic) dictionaries available in the market at present are full of errors. The textbooks prescribed in the schools and English language centers in the Middle East are totally ignoring this important aspect of communication.

1.3 Objectives of the Study

The key aims and objectives of this study are to explore common pronunciation difficulties that are faced by Arabic speakers when they learn to speak English. The researcher aims to identify major difficulties and find out the root causes behind these difficulties. The findings regarding the underlying causes of these difficulties were utilized by the researcher to present recommendations and solutions to overcome those difficulties. Effective communication is a key to success in all areas of human endeavours. For any successful transaction or business operation, it is imperative that the sender is successful in communicating the message to the intended receiver. Errors in pronunciation may affect the quality of the message, and the receiver may not exactly understand the message. Hence it is extremely important to concentrate on the pronunciation and correct it to come as close as possible to that of the native speaker.

1.4 Significance of the Study

The pronunciation of the English language is very difficult to learn for native Arabic speakers. There may be several factors responsible for this phenomenon. This study identifies those factors and presents solutions to overcome those difficulties. These are useful guidelines and recommendations for native Arabic speakers in particular and English learners in general. It will help them to know these causes in advance and apply the remedial measures to make their learning experience as result-oriented as possible.

It will increase their learning curve, and they will have a sense of direction regarding how pronunciation learning should be approached in the case of the English language. It will also assist organizations that send their employees for English learning courses. They will be able to identify the most appropriate courses and the best learning resources to remove the deficiencies of their staff. Finally, it will also assist organizations that plan and offer English language courses to adjust their course content to the needs of the participants.

1.5 Definition of Key Terms

Pronunciation

Pronunciation is the correct way of saying a word. It also refers to a graphic representation, using phonetic symbols, of the way a word is spoken.

Pronunciation Difficulties

Problems encountered in saying a word in the correct way by the learners of the language.

Native Speakers

Someone who has spoken a particular language since they were a baby, rather than having learned it as a child or adult. A native speaker of a language is someone who speaks that language as their first language rather than having learned it as a foreign language.

Native Arabic Speakers

People who speak Arabic as their first language and have spoken Arabic since their earliest childhood.

CHAPTER 2

LITERATURE REVIEW

Common English Errors by Arabic Speakers

Arabic and English are two very different languages in terms of writing system and direction of writing. Cummins,[1] in the 1980s, came up with the idea that a second language can be learned easily if the person attains command of the native language. The knowledge and skills acquired in mastering the native language form the basis of learning the second language (Palmer et al. 2007). However, Arabic letters are different than English letters. They are written in a right-to-left direction, whereas English is written in a left-to-right direction. Also, Arabic is a consonant-heavy language. In the written form, vowels are not much emphasized and often omitted. As a result, when Arabic speakers learn English, they tend to exchange or reassign vowels (Miller 2012, p. n.d).

---

[1] Professor J. Cummins is a well-known authority on second language learning.

Following are some specific difficulties that Arabic speakers face in learning English:

Adjectives

In the Arabic language, the adjective comes after the noun. Arabic speakers tend to simulate this construct while learning English such as "The cat white" or "The house small" (Miller 2012, p. n.d).

Vowels

The English language contains twenty vowel sounds. On the contrary, the Arabic language has only eight vowel sounds. Hence Arabic speakers find it difficult to understand and use vowels in English. Common errors in vowels include *bet/bat* or *ball/bell* (Miller 2012, p. n.d).

Stress

In Arabic, there is no stress on words. All words and syllables are spoken in the same manner without any emphasis. This leads to many pronunciation problems while learning English. The pronunciation of the English language emphasizes stress on individual syllables (Miller 2012, p. n.d).

Writing

Arabic is written right to left, whereas English is written left to right. The vowels are often omitted, depending on the pattern of consonants and the context of the discourse. Punctuation rules are very flexible in the Arabic language. There is no differentiation of upper-case and lower-case letters in the Arabic language.

Unfortunately, Arabic students carry these behaviours with them when learning English. This causes difficulties and issues for them (Miller 2012, p. n.d).

Learning Resources

There are many resources available that can improve English pronunciation and accent. The first such resource is books or guides on the English language. Books and guides can also be rented from a local library. There are books dedicated to the pronunciation of the English alphabet and structure. Examples include *American English Pronunciation* by Donna Hope, *English Pronunciation in Use Elementary* by Jonathan Marks, *English Pronunciation in Use Advanced* by Martin Hewings, and *Transcribing the Sound of English: A Phonetics Workbook for Words and Discourse* by Paul Tench (Hope 2006; Marks 2007; Hewings 2010; Tench 2011).

There are also websites that offer lessons on the English language. These websites include EnglishLearner.com, TalkEnglish.com, and World-English.org. English Learner websites offer listening exercises at beginner, intermediate, and advanced levels (Mathe 2013, p. n.d). The Talk English website offers lessons on reading, speaking, and listening. The lessons are structured in three steps: identify, understand, and integrate (Talk English 2013, p. n.d). The World English website is a huge resource of English language activities, exercises, and tests. It contains online English lessons, online phonetics, and English tongue twisters (World English 2004, p. n.d).

Another option is to register for an online service that offers English accent training and improvement classes. Some websites offer free online services such as ToLearnEnglish.com. The features in this website include placement tests, lessons and exercises, a club, leisure time, and specialized tools (ToLearnEnglish 2013, p. n.d). There are also various software programs for learning correct accent and pronunciation, such as Rosetta Stone. It has named its learning methodology dynamic immersion. This methodology activates natural language learning ability and uses the intuitive approach for teaching the English language (Rosetta Stone 2013, p. n.d).

Another method to improve pronunciation is to read rhyming poetry aloud. An example is Dr. Seuss's children's books. Reading tongue twisters that focus on specific sounds as well as reading other poetry in a loud voice makes those who are studying the language fall into the rhythm of the language. This immersion builds pronunciation at the heart that it becomes difficult to mispronounce those words in the future. Such knowledge will carry over to non-rhyming material, and overall conversation will improve (Basilicato 2013, p. n.d).

English Pronunciation Rules

English pronunciation rules are considered arbitrary and inconsistent, to say the least. There are many examples of pronunciation that show that consistency is not maintained in English pronunciation. The word *cough* does not rhyme with the words *bough* and *tough*. The word *heard* rhymes with the word *bird*; however, it does not rhyme with the word *beard*. Despite these discrepancies, English pronunciation is not without rules, and there are various rules present for assisting in the correct pronunciation of the English language (Basilicato 2013, p. n.d).

The pronunciation for *c* is the hard sound of the *k*. Examples are *car*, *cat*, and *candy*. When *e*, *i*, or *y* follows *c*, the pronunciation is the soft sound of the *s*. Examples are *publicist*, *cycle*, and *cedar*. When *e*, *i*, or *y* follows *g*, the pronunciation is the soft sound of the *j*. Examples are *gym*, *magic*, and *generous*. When *e* occurs at the end of the word, the effect on the pronunciation is a long sound to the preceding vowel. Examples are *sham/shame, hat/hate, not/note, ton/tone, kit/kite*. When *a* follows *w*, the sound is like a short *o*. An example is *watch*. When *o* follows *w*, the sound is like a short *u*. An example is *worry* (Basilicato 2013, p. n.d).

There are also silent letters in the English pronunciation. Some silent combinations are identified very easily. This is because the words are otherwise difficult to pronounce. Examples are *light, fight, daughter, autumn*, and *hymn*. In other cases, it is difficult to identify the silent letter. Examples are silent *e* in the middle of words such as *every, evening*, or *temperature*. Other silent letters are *b, l, h*, and *kn*. Examples include *climb, thumb, talk, half, honest, hour, knight, knife*, and *knock* (Basilicato 2013, p. n.d).

Phonetic Differences

English and Arabic languages originate from two different families of languages. English originates from the Germanic family, whereas Arabic originates from the Semitic family. Since they originate from different families of languages, both English and Arabic speakers find it difficult to learn Arabic and English respectively. Calculate the amount of vowel phonemes and differences between English and Arabic. The grammar of a language also includes its phonetic attributes. In these phonetic attributes as well, there are many differences between the English and the Arabic languages (Payne 2013, p. n.d).

Individual Sounds

Speech sounds are different from the letters of the alphabet of the language. In language terminology, speech sounds are known as phonemes. The consonants in the English alphabet are twenty. However, consonant phonemes in the English alphabet are twenty-four. The vowels in the English alphabet are six. However, vowel phonemes in the English language are twenty. In the Arabic language, consonant phonemes are twenty-eight and vowel phonemes are eight. Hence, when we compare the English language with the Arabic language, we find that there are four more consonant phonemes and fourteen less vowel phonemes. Hence, the Arabic language is a consonant-heavy language as compared to the English language (Payne 2013, p. n.d).

The BBC website also provides a chart for the sounds of English. This chart is given below:

Table 2: Sounds of English

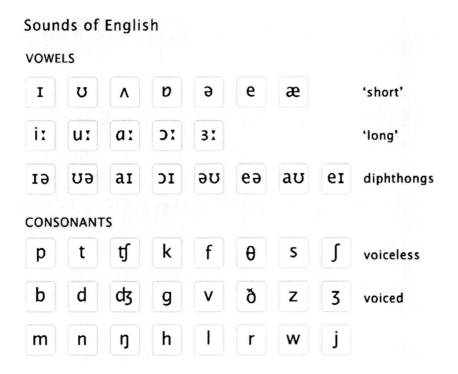

Sounds of English

VOWELS

| I | ʊ | ʌ | ɒ | ə | e | æ | | 'short' |

| iː | uː | ɑː | ɔː | ɜː | | | | 'long' |

| Iə | ʊə | aɪ | ɔɪ | əʊ | eə | aʊ | eɪ | diphthongs |

CONSONANTS

| p | t | tʃ | k | f | θ | s | ʃ | voiceless |

| b | d | dʒ | g | v | ð | z | ʒ | voiced |

| m | n | ŋ | h | l | r | w | j | |

Source: **BBC, 2013.**

Sound Combinations

There are also numerous differences in sound combinations in the Arabic and the English language. The grouping of phonemes is referred to as consonant clusters. English has many more words with consonant clusters than Arabic. Arabic has two-consonant clusters but no three-consonant clusters. English has numerous three-consonant and even four-consonant clusters such as "*first*," "*twelveth*," and *"schlock."* Hence Arabic speakers find it difficult to pronounce these clusters. For example, they might pronounce *next* as *nexist* (Payne 2013, p. n.d).

Word Stress

In Arabic, there is no word stress, and each word and syllable is pronounced in the same manner. In English, word stress is considered very important, and it can even alter the meaning and lexical category of a word. For example, *ob-jéct* is a verb in the English language. However, *ób-ject* is a noun in the English language (Payne 2013, p. n.d).

Sound Elision

There is no sound elision in the Arabic language; however, this is a common phonetic feature in the English language. Elision means dropping a sound in the middle of or between the words. This is done in order to verbalise a phrase or a sentence. Examples of elision are *cap'n/captain, wanna/want to*. In Arabic, spelling closely resembles the sound. Hence sounds are rarely omitted (Payne 2013, p. n.d).

Phonetic Transcriptions

There are various systems for writing phonetic transcriptions of English words. Amongst these, the International Phonetic Alphabet (IPA) is the most popular system. It is used in dictionaries, *Wikipedia*, and many academic books. The major disadvantage of this method is that it uses certain special symbols like ə or ɔ that cannot be easily typed on computers (Szynalski 2013, p. n.d).

There are two major problems in IPA format. The first problem is that not all fonts support IPA symbols. However, there is at least one font in all modern operating systems that supports IPA symbols. Also, many applications allow font substitution, which allows borrowing of the font. The borrowed characters will not resemble the look and style of the current font, but they will be readable. However, the best results are obtained when IPA-enabled font is used. Modern operating systems have various IPA-enabled fonts. Windows XP includes Lucida Sans Unicode font. Windows Vista includes Segoe UI, Arial, Times New Roman, Tahoma, and Lucida Sans Unicode fonts. Windows 7 and 8 include Segoe UI, Cambria, Calibri, Arial, Times New Roman, Tahoma, and Lucida Sans Unicode fonts. OS X includes Lucida Grande, Arial, Times New Roman, and Tahoma fonts. Linux includes Linux Libertine, Linux Biolinum, and DejaVu Sans fonts (IPA 2013, p. n.d).

Another problem with IPA symbols is that usually keyboard shortcuts are not available for them. There have been two solutions devised to address this issue. One solution is to use the TypeIt app for Windows. Using TypeIt involves three steps. First, the TypeIt program is executed. Second, a TypeIt keyboard is selected from the drop-down list. Third, the IPA symbols are typed, and the Send button is clicked. Clicking Send inserts these symbols into the document (TypeIt 2013). A second solution is to make use of the IPA website, Ipa.TypeIt.org. This website provides a keyboard for typing IPA phonetic symbols. The written text can then be copied into the word processor in use by the writer (Szynalski 2013, p. n.d).

IPA symbols can also be avoided altogether. There is also an alternative transcription system made. This system was developed by Tomasz P. Szynalski and Michal Ryszard Wojcik in the 1990s. The system is known as the ASCII Phonetic Alphabet. ASCII stands for American standard code for information interchange. It is a character encoding scheme. It encodes 128 characters. These include upper-case letters *A* to *Z*, lower-case letters *a* to *z*, numbers *0* to *9*, certain punctuation symbols, and several control codes. The ASCII Phonetic Alphabet system uses ASCII characters instead of special IPA symbols. This makes it easy for typing them on computers, because all ASCII characters are available on computers. A comparison of both systems is shown below:

Table 3: Vowel symbols

IPA	ASCII
ʌ	^
ɑː	aː
Æ	@
E	E
ə	..
ɜːʳ	eː(r)
ɪ	I
iː	iː
ɒ	O
ɔː	oː
ʊ	U
uː	uː
aɪ	Ai

aʊ	Au
eɪ	Ei
oʊ	Ou
ɔɪ	Oi
eəʳ	e..(r)
ɪəʳ	i..(r)
ʊəʳ	u..(r)

Source: **Szynalski, 2013.**

Table 4: Consonant symbols

IPA	ASCII
B	b
D	d
F	f
G	g
H	h
J	j
K	k

L	l
M	m
N	n
ŋ	N
P	p
R	r
S	s
ʃ	S
T	t
tʃ	tS
Θ	th
Ð	TH
V	v
W	w
Z	z
ʒ	Z
dʒ	dZ

Source: **Szynalski, 2013.**

Table 5: Special symbols

IPA	ASCII
'	,
r	(r)
i	i(:)
$^{\ni}$l	.l
$^{\ni}$n	.n

Source: Szynalski, 2013.

CHAPTER 3

METHODOLOGY

3.1 *Research Framework*

The framework for this study is a descriptive research, and it answers questions concerning the current status of the subject of the study. The research collects data related to the pronunciation difficulties for native Arabic speakers and presents findings and recommendations after analysing the data and identifying key themes of the topic.

3.2 *Research Method*

Most research studies represent a readily identifiable method. All studies have certain procedures in common such as the statement of a problem, collection of data, and drawing of conclusions. Beyond these, however, specific procedures are of too high a degree to be determined by the research method. Each of the methods is designed to answer a different type of question. The five categories of research methods are historical, descriptive, correlational, causal comparative, and experimental.

Historical research involves studying, understanding, and explaining past events. The purpose is to arrive at conclusions concerning causes, effects, or trends of past occurrences that may help to explain present events and anticipate future events. Historical researchers do not typically gather data by administering instruments to individuals. They seek out data already available.

Descriptive research involves collecting data in order to test hypotheses or to answer questions concerning the current status of the subject of the study. A high percentage of reported research studies is descriptive. The descriptive method is useful for investigating and analysing a variety of business and management problems. Typical descriptive studies are concerned with the assessment of attitudes, opinions, demographic information, conditions, and procedures. Descriptive data is usually collected through a questionnaire, survey, interview, observation, or some combination of these methods.

Correlational research primarily describes an existing condition. The condition it describes, however, is distinctly different from the conditions typically described in a self-report or observational studies. A correlational study describes in quantitative terms the degree to which variables are related. Correlational research involves collecting data in order to determine whether and to what degree a relationship exists between two or more quantifiable variables. The degree of relationship is expressed as a correlation coefficient. A relationship may exist between two variables in such a way that a low score accompanies higher scores on one than the other or vice versa. For example, there is a relationship between intelligence and academic achievement. Persons who do well in intelligence tests tend to have a higher grade point average. Persons who do poorly in intelligence tests tend to have a lower grade point average. It means that there is a relationship between the two measures. Correlational studies also provide an estimate of the level of relationship between two variables. If two variables are strongly related, a correlational coefficient of +1.00 or −1.00 will be obtained. If two variables are not related, a coefficient of 0.00 will be obtained. Relationships are rarely perfect. However, sufficiently related variables permit useful predictions.

In causal comparative research, the researcher attempts to determine the cause or reason for existing differences in the behaviour or status of groups of individuals. The researcher attempts to identify the major factor leading to this difference. The researcher attempts to identify the effects and study the causes that have already occurred. The basic causal comparative study starts with identifying an effect and seeks its possible causes. The causal comparative studies identify cause–effect relationships involving two or more groups and one independent variable. Moreover, these studies involve comparison.

In an experimental study, the researcher manipulates at least one variable and observes the effect on one or more dependent variables. Manipulation of the independent variable is the one single characteristic that differentiates experimental research from other methods. In experimental research, the groups to be studied are randomly formed before the experiment, a procedure not involved in other methods of research. The sense of experimentation is control. The researcher strives to ensure that the experiences of the groups are equal on all important variables except the independent variable. If at the end of some period of time, groups differ in performance on the dependent variable, the difference can be attributed to the independent variable. It is important to understand that because of the direct manipulations and control of variables, experimental research is the only type of research that can truly establish a cause–effect relationship.

The research method for this study is descriptive. The researcher collected data to determine the common pronunciation difficulties among native Arabic speakers learning and speaking English. The research used a mixed method approach, being qualitative–quantitative. On the qualitative part, the researcher identified and presented key themes as they relate to pronunciation difficulties. On the quantitative part, the researcher sought to test and confirm the qualitative findings and presented these findings in tabular form.

The study also relies on both primary and secondary data. For collecting primary data, the researcher developed two questionnaires. The first questionnaire was related to phonological difficulties of native Arabic speakers. The second questionnaire was a quiz about the English pronunciation. The sample size of the study was fifty, and these fifty participants filled the two questionnaires for the study. For collecting secondary data, the researcher read various articles related to the importance of English pronunciation, how to learn English pronunciation, English pronunciation activities, English pronunciation rules, and common errors observed in English pronunciation. The researcher also studied specific difficulties of native Arabic speakers.

3.3 Research Data

The data for this research is a combination of various collections and types of data.

Data Collected through Survey 1

The first survey was related to phonological difficulties of native Arabic speakers. The participants had a list of English letters or sounds that Arabic speakers typically have difficulty pronouncing or distinguishing. Participants had to respond if they still had difficulty in distinguishing these letters or sounds or if they had overcome the difficulty in the process of their learning the language. Participants were also asked to mention the learning methodology for learning the pronunciation. The survey form is as follows:

SURVEY: Phonological Difficulties of Native Arabic Speakers

I want you to think back on your experience learning/teaching English. What are some of the difficulties you encountered with your students or your students themselves in learning the pronunciation of the new words and learning to say new sounds not evident in the Arabic language?

Below is a chart that lists some of the vital English letters and sounds that Arabic speakers must learn to pronounce and distinguish between in order to speak English properly. Please complete the charts with any other letters/sounds/words that you know native Arabic speakers find challenging or may have difficulty with.

Identifying Phonological Difficulties among Native Arabic Speakers

Overcame	Still have difficulty	Distinguish letters or sounds	Examples of words	Approach/ technique used in learning the pronunciation
		/p/ and /b/	*pen* and *ben*	
		/e/ and /i/	*sit* and *set*	

		/o/ and /u/	*sock* and *suck*	
		/g/ and /j/	*get* and *jet*	
		/f/ and /v/	*fail* and *veil*	
		/r/	trilling of the *r*	
		/x/	*expect*	
		/l/ velar (hard) stress not only when followed by a consonant	*light* (as in *milk*)	
		/ch/ as /sh/	*cheat* and *sheet*	
		/ng/	*sing* with a stress on *g* as in *egg*	

		Some words with a silent *e* followed by an *s*	*clothes* as a two-syllable word /clo-thes/	

Please complete the first two columns, "Overcame" and "Still Have Difficulty," only if you are a native speaker of Arabic.

1. Place a check in the column "Overcame" to indicate the letters or sounds/examples of words that you now pronounce correctly with little or no difficulty.

2. Note in the column "Approach/Technique Used in Learning the Pronunciation," all method(s) that apply in acquiring said pronunciation.

3. Place a check in the column "Still Have Difficulty" to indicate the letters or sounds / examples of words that you still have difficulty pronouncing correctly.

Data Collected through Survey 2

The second survey was a quiz about the English pronunciation. The questions were closed-ended, and participants had to select between the two options. There were ten questions of the quiz. They were related to pronunciation, rhyme, and sounds. The quiz is as follows:

A Quiz about the English Pronunciation

1. Are the words *son* and *sun* pronounced the same way?

    Yes

    No

2. Does the word *basic* have an *s* or *z* sound?

    s

    z

3. Does the word *school* rhyme with *fool*?

    Yes

    No

4. Does the word *cheese* have an *s* or *z* sound?

    s

    z

5. Does the word *any* rhyme with *penny* or *nanny*?

    penny

    nanny

6. Does the word *of* have an *f* sound or a *v* sound?

    f

    v

7. Does the word *low* rhyme with *throw*?

    Yes

    No

8. Are the words *row* and *raw* pronounced the same way?

    Yes

    No

9. Does the word *food* rhyme with *good*?

     Yes

     No

10. Are the words *roll* and *role* pronounced the same way?

     Yes

     No

Thank you for your valuable assistance.

Answers to the Quiz about the English Pronunciation

1. Are the words *son* and *sun* pronounced the same way?

   Yes, both are pronounced /sun/.

2. Does the word *basic* have an *s* or *z* sound?

   S. It is pronounced /bā´-sik/.

3. Does the word *school* rhyme with *fool*?

   Yes, *school* is pronounced /skool/ and fool is pronounced /fool/.

4. Does the word *cheese* have an *s* or *z* sound?

   Z. It is pronounced /chēz/.

5. Does the word *any* rhyme with *penny* or *nanny*?

   Penny. Any is pronounced /en´-ē /. *Penny* is pronounced /pen´-ē/, and *nanny* is pronounced /nan´-ē/.

6. Does the word *of* have an *f* sound or a *v* sound?

   V. It is pronounced /uv/.

7. Does the word *low* rhyme with *throw*?

    Yes, *low* is pronounced /lō/, and *throw* is pronounced /thrō/.

8. Are the words *row* and *raw* pronounced the same way?

    No, *row* is pronounced /rō/, and *raw* is pronounced /rô/.

9. Does the word *food* rhyme with *good*?

    No, *food* is pronounced /food/, and *good* is pronounced /good/.

10. Are the words *roll* and *role* pronounced the same way?

    Yes, they are both pronounced /rōl/.

Data Collected through Reading

The two main types of data are primary data and secondary data. Primary data is collected for the project at hand, while secondary data has been collected earlier for some other problems or projects, and it can later be used for making a decision if found suitable for the purpose, other than the original one. Secondary data can be acquired from institutions, organizations, and from other external sources such as academic institutions, governments, and professional consultants, subject to the availability of data and their respective policies for making data accessible. Some of the government and semi-government agencies and autonomous bodies collect data and make it accessible to users on request.

It is advisable to always search for available data. The use of secondary data can reduce the cost of the research project and also facilitates earlier completion of the project. Secondary data is usually available in published form comprising of books, periodicals, and other documents available in libraries and educational institutions and may also be available via Internet, that is, by netnography (Kozinet 2010). A few days' labour to search for the desired information from published and unpublished material could avoid the need for many weeks of lengthy interviews and elaborate surveys, thereby reducing the completion time of the project and its associated cost. Research studies requiring comparisons can be easily completed on time with more accurate secondary data and reliable information obtained from published annual reports, assessment records, etc.

The disadvantage is that information or data collected earlier for a problem might not match totally with the situation. The secondary data should be used cautiously, after seeking necessary permission. If government agencies, academic institutions, associations, or other sources provide data of acceptable quality at a lower cost, it is obviously proper to use those alternatives. Frequently, the data provided by such organizations is superior to the data a private firm could secure in its own research. However, mistrust and the level of inaccuracy would increase if the secondary source data were used instead of the secondary data. There is a need to distinguish between the two terms, secondary data and secondary sources. Data collected by someone else is secondary data. If the researcher obtains secondary data from the party who collected them, he is using an original or primary source. If secondary data is taken from a source that obtained them from the original source, then a secondary source is being used. It is important to avoid the use of secondary sources. Wherever possible, only the original sources for secondary data should be used.

In case secondary data sought is not available from reliable sources, the researcher will have to collect primary data. The next step is to collect primary data, but first it needs to be determined who has the desired information and how it can be obtained. The researcher must decide whether the data is to be collected through the survey or observational or experimental methods. Since the methodology used by the party for collecting the secondary data is not explained, the accuracy level of the secondary data would not be verified. It is, therefore, essential to be more careful in interpretation of such quality data, and omissions, if they occur, need to be reflected in the final analysis and findings of the report, as when secondary data is used for making any inferences or drawing conclusions.

The researcher also collects data through reading of various journals, articles, magazines, and other web resources. Hence, this research study relies on both primary and secondary data.

3.4 Research Instruments

Survey research is vital for collecting primary data. Survey means to look over, to examine conditions and situations to appraise value. To carry out these activities, the researcher has to identify and directly source the data, either by taking on a participatory role on site or by contacting relevant people through face-to-face visits or through some other medium of communication, such as telephone or emails and/or otherwise accessing records or other pertinent documents and materials for analysis.

A survey is the method predominately used for collecting primary data in formal research. In using this instrument to obtain primary data, a researcher may prepare a formal questionnaire, which might be delivered to the respondents for them to fill out independently to be collected back on a later date, or they may complete them at the time of delivery with the assistance of the researcher. Questionnaires that are to be filled out independently by respondents have to be properly designed and easy to understand without ambiguities and clearly explaining the content and data required. A survey could also take the form of personal interviews, which the researcher conducts with the help of a questionnaire or interview schedule, or it could otherwise take the form of a focus group made up of a number of people gathered together. The interviews may be structured or unstructured, depending on the type and quality of data required.

In business and social research, having knowledge of the real reasons for certain behaviours that a respondent would not wish to disclose or for decisions that are a result of something that exists in their subconscious can be very important. A questionnaire, therefore, should not include those questions that the respondents are not likely to answer or would not answer truthfully. Instead, they would need to be substituted for other questions that respondents would be more comfortable answering, the results of which could still provide some insight into the behaviour being researched. Qualitative methods, though not fully scientific, are valued for giving directions in disclosing the cause of such behaviour. The qualitative method involves finding out what people think. It also lays great emphasis on knowing people's feelings. In other words, in qualitative research, the emphasis is on investigating feelings and impressions, rather than numbers. Qualitative research has continued to develop as a instrument in investigating and enhancing knowledge about the real reasons for certain types of behaviour among members of society.

In contrast, quantitative research provides information to which numbers can be applied and statistics can be derived. Such data is useful not only for assessing and measuring what may be happening at a particular point in time, but when combined with historical and other data, it can be useful in forecasting and establishing patterns and trends. Business and social organizations today are just as interested in knowing not only what and how but also why. Therefore, the mixed method, which combines the benefits of both types of research, can provide even more valuable insight into people's behaviour. Thus they are both important for decision-makers in business as well as in social institutions to provide necessary data for making effective decisions.

This research uses a mixed method, applying both quantitative and qualitative methods in order to achieve the objective of this dissertation. Its questionnaires have included closed-ended as well as open-ended questions in order to assess common difficulties, while at the same time allowing participants the opportunity to volunteer any additional information that they considered relevant to the research. The researcher has been able to present the findings numerically based on present key themes of the research.

3.5 Scope and Research Location

3.5.1 Scope

Learning the English language is a very broad topic. There are various factors, issues, and themes involved. To have a meaningful analysis and focused research, the researcher defined a clear scope for the study. This study focused its attention on analysing only the difficulties related to the pronunciation of the English language. There are difficulties to learning related to grammar as well as vocabulary, but this was not covered in this study. It focused its efforts towards the analysis of pronunciation difficulties only. Also, all those who do not have English as their first language find some kind of difficulty in learning to write and speak English. However, this study focused on the phonological issues of native Arabic speakers only.

3.5.2 Research Location

The research targets English language learners living in Middle Eastern countries. The respondents belonged to one of the countries of the Middle East and were native Arabic speakers.

3.6 Data Collection Technique

A sample is a subset or a part of a larger population. The purpose of sampling is to infer or estimate some unknown and representative characteristics of the target population. A sample has to be a representative of the population. If drawn on a random basis, it can provide accurate data about the target population. Majority of research studies collect data through samples to keep the cost, time, and quality of research under control by preparing a more reliable and representative sample design for studying the target population. Sample designs must be such that the data collected through sampling units should be helpful in achieving the objectives of the research project for studying the problem. When data is collected through a sample as opposed to a census, the user of the data should be vigilant that sampling errors will be there, and sampling errors can be calculated from summary information or mean values, percentages, and proportions.

There are two ways of selecting a sample, random or non-random sampling. They are also known as probability and non-probability sampling respectively. A random sample can be a stratified, systematic, or area sample. In random sampling, each element that makes up the population has a known chance of being selected as a sample. In non-random sampling, the sample is not determined by chance. Their selection is based on the choice and judgement of the researcher. Those units that are selected are thought of as good representative samples. The most significant difference between the random and non-random sampling is that the statistical inference can be drawn only from the random sampling methods. Random or probability sampling methods have been developed on the basis of a number of theories and concepts of mathematics and statistics.

This research uses a non-random sampling method. Non-random sampling methods are of three types: convenience sampling, judgement sampling, and quota sampling. In convenience sampling, the researcher seeks a response in the questionnaire to appraise its value as an instrument for facilitating the communication between two people. Convenience samples are often used in exploratory studies to get an approximate estimate of the actual values inexpensively and speedily. Judgement sampling is used when specialists or persons with certain experiences are qualified to provide information, then such persons are included in the sample. Quota sampling is a form of stratified sampling. It differs from stratified random sampling only in the manner of selecting the sample units. The selection of sample units involves the judgement of someone. Often the researcher defines the criteria for selection.

The sample for this research was selected through judgement sampling. The researcher visited various English language teaching institutes and used his judgement to identify people who could respond to the questions in the survey. The researcher thus identified seventy-four participants for this study, of which fifty responded.

3.6.1 Data Collected from People

There were two survey questionnaires for this study; Survey 1 was related to phonological difficulties of native Arabic speakers. Survey 2 was a quiz about English pronunciation. The research provided these two survey questionnaires to the research participants.

They were asked to fill these questionnaires at their own convenience and return the questionnaires back to the researcher within two weeks of their receipt.

3.6.2 Data Collected from Documents

The researcher also collected secondary data through various newspapers, articles, books, and other web sources. He consolidated the data to form the key themes of the study. These themes will be presented in chapter 4 of the dissertation.

CHAPTER 4

ANALYSIS

This research relied on both primary and secondary data. In the primary research, it had both quantitative and qualitative analysis of the data. The findings and results of the study are as follows:

Different Dialects of the English Language

The English language, like many other languages, has different dialects. Pronunciation is defined as the correct way of speaking a word in the language. However, when there are different dialects in a language, it becomes very difficult to identify what the standard pronunciation is. For example, some English speakers elongate vowels while speaking. Some English speakers have a nasal pronunciation to many words. These include New York state residents and Midwestern United States residents. African Americans cut words short in phrases. Other speakers do not distinguish between vowel sounds. Hence *this* is pronounced the same as the word *these* (Saylor 2012,

p. n.d). This adds to the difficulties of a native Arabic speaker who wants to learn to speak English. He not only has to have a grip on the correct pronunciation but also needs to know that there are different dialects of the language in addition to what is considered standard English. In the Middle East and in most other non-English speaking countries, standard English falls in two categories, namely American English and British English. The non-native speaker will need to decide which form of standard English is the most appropriate in his context and situation.

Effects of Poor Pronunciation

Poor pronunciation distorts the quality of the message. It is feared that the recipient may not fully understand what the sender needs to convey in his message. However, use of the local accent has its advantages too. It becomes easier for people of the same nationality to understand each other's accent when speaking English. For example, when an Englishman talks English in his own accent, an Indian person might find it difficult to understand the words. However, when an Indian speaks English to another Indian, it can be comprehended easily because of the local accent.

Also, if a business has a focus around a particular country or a particular nationality, the local accent of that country may prove useful. Consider the example of a French restaurant in the United States. A French person who can speak English might be preferred because it is more likely that his accent will be understood by the mostly French visitors to the restaurant. Also, the local accent could provide a benefit of doubt to the sender of the message. The recipient of the message knows that the person is not a native speaker of the language and the words should not be taken at face value. If there is any harshness or negative connotation found in the words, it may be because of the person's poor command of the language, and he actually did not mean it. On the contrary, if a person masters the pronunciation of the English language, he will be treated just like the native speaker, and any omissions and errors on his part may not be forgiven.

Contributing Factors for Correct Pronunciation

There are several factors that, when mastered together, enable the student to utter correct pronunciation. These factors include correct sound of the word, loud and clear volume of the word, and pitch of the word.

Learning Pronunciation through Practice

English is a language spoken worldwide in business and in academic pursuits. Hence, it is important for non-native people to learn the language as a tool for communication and knowledge assimilation. English is not an especially phonetic language. A word may be spelled out in one way and said in another way. Pronunciation becomes very difficult when foreigners try to learn the English language. Hence, it is important to learn the pronunciation by practising and listening to English phrases. It is important that students of English language are patient and diligent in their efforts. There are various methodologies that can be adopted to learn English pronunciation.

Difference between Arabic and English

There are numerous differences in the approaches of Arabic and English language. This is a major reason native Arabic speakers who are learning English or who have learned English find it difficult to learn to speak English. Arabic letters are different from English letters. They are written in a right-to-left direction, whereas English is written in a left-to-right direction. In the Arabic language, the adjective comes after the noun. In Arabic, there is no stress on words. All words and syllables are spoken in the same manner without any emphasis. Punctuation rules are very flexible in the Arabic language. There is no differentiation of upper-case and lower-case letters. There is also no sound elision in the Arabic language.

English and Arabic languages originate from two different families of languages. English originates from the Germanic family, whereas Arabic originates from the Semitic family. The consonants in the English alphabet are twenty. However, consonant phonemes in the English alphabet are twenty-four. The vowels in the English alphabet are six. However, vowel phonemes in the English language are twenty (see table 3). In the Arabic language, consonant phonemes are twenty-eight, and vowel phonemes are eight. Hence, when we compare the English language with the Arabic language, we find that there are four more consonant phonemes and fourteen less vowel phonemes. Hence, the Arabic language is a consonant-heavy language as compared to the English language.

There are also numerous differences in sound combinations in the Arabic and the English language. The grouping of phonemes is referred to as consonant clusters. English has many more consonant clusters for forming words than Arabic. Arabic has two-consonant clusters but no three-consonant clusters. English has numerous three-consonant and even four-consonant clusters. Hence Arabic speakers find it difficult to pronounce these clusters.

Responses of Survey 1

Fifty participants out of sixty-five filled out the survey and returned it to the researcher. It was decided to eliminate from the analysis the last pronunciation difficulty identified in Survey 1 because on reviewing the completed survey, it was discovered that most respondents misunderstood what was required for this last question in the table. It may have been poorly worded and is actually dissimilar in type and general tenor of the other difficult phonemes, which resulted in some confusion among participants.

Participants were given mostly sample pairs of letters or sounds. They were asked if they had overcome the difficulty in pronouncing these letters or sounds or if they still had difficulty. The results are summarized below. In the table below, P1 stands for participant 1; P2 stands for participant 2, and so on. Similarly S1 stands for the first sample of letters or sounds provided, S2 stands for the second sample of letters or sounds provided, and so on. At the end of the table, the frequency of each sample is mentioned as to how many responded that had overcome the difficulty and how many still found it difficult to pronounce certain letters.

Table 6: Survey 1 results

Participant/ sample	S1	S2	S3	S4	S5	S6	S7	S8	S9	S10
P1	O	D	O	O	D	D	D	D	D	D
P2	D	O	D	O	O	D	D	D	D	O
P3	D	D	D	O	D	O	D	O	D	D
P4	D	O	D	O	D	D	D	D	O	D
P5	D	D	O	D	O	D	O	D	D	D
P6	D	D	O	O	D	D	D	D	O	O
P7	O	O	D	D	D	O	D	D	O	D
P8	D	D	D	O	O	D	D	D	D	D
P9	D	D	O	D	D	D	D	D	D	D
P10	D	D	O	D	D	D	D	D	D	D
P11	O	D	D	O	O	D	D	D	D	D
P12	D	D	D	D	D	O	D	D	D	D
P13	D	D	D	O	O	D	D	D	D	O
P14	D	D	D	O	D	D	D	D	O	D
P15	D	D	O	D	O	D	O	D	D	D
P16	D	D	D	O	D	D	D	O	D	D

Participant/ sample	S1	S2	S3	S4	S5	S6	S7	S8	S9	S10
P17	D	D	O	O	O	D	D	D	D	O
P18	D	D	D	O	D	O	D	D	D	D
P19	D	O	O	O	D	D	D	D	O	D
P20	D	D	D	O	O	D	D	D	O	O
P21	D	D	O	D	D	D	D	D	D	D
P22	O	O	D	D	D	D	D	D	D	D
P23	D	O	D	D	O	D	O	D	O	D
P24	D	D	O	O	O	D	D	D	O	D
P25	D	D	O	O	O	D	O	D	O	D
P26	D	O	D	O	D	O	D	D	D	D
P27	D	D	D	O	D	D	D	O	D	D
P28	D	D	O	D	D	D	D	D	D	D
P29	D	D	O	D	D	D	D	D	D	D
P30	D	D	D	O	O	D	D	D	D	D
P31	O	O	D	O	D	D	D	D	D	D
P32	D	O	D	D	O	O	D	D	D	D
P33	D	D	D	O	D	D	D	O	D	D
P34	O	D	O	O	D	D	D	D	O	O

Participant/ sample	S1	S2	S3	S4	S5	S6	S7	S8	S9	S10
P35	D	D	O	D	O	D	D	D	D	D
P36	D	D	D	O	D	D	D	D	O	D
P37	D	D	O	O	D	O	D	D	O	D
P38	D	D	O	D	D	D	O	D	D	D
P39	D	D	O	O	D	D	D	D	D	O
P40	D	O	D	D	D	O	D	D	D	D
P41	O	D	O	O	D	D	D	D	D	D
P42	D	O	D	D	D	D	D	D	D	D
P43	O	D	O	D	O	O	D	D	O	D
P44	D	D	D	O	D	D	D	D	D	O
P45	D	D	D	O	D	D	D	D	O	O
P46	O	O	O	D	D	O	D	D	D	O
P47	O	D	O	D	D	D	D	O	O	D
P48	D	O	O	O	D	D	D	D	D	D
P49	D	O	O	D	D	D	D	D	D	D
P50	D	O	O	O	D	D	D	D	D	D
Overcame	10	15	25	30	15	10	5	5	15	10
Difficulty	40	35	25	20	35	40	45	45	35	40

From the table, it is evident that native Arabic speakers have many difficulties in their pronunciation and, in spite of their formal learning, have not been able to resolve their issues. This led the researcher to seek out what sources are available for learning English pronunciation.

Learning Resources

There are many learning resources available to improve and correct English pronunciation. Book resources include *American English Pronunciation* by Donna Hope, *English Pronunciation in Use Elementary* by Jonathan Marks, *English Pronunciation in Use Advanced* by Martin Hewings, and *Transcribing the Sound of English: A Phonetics Workbook for Words and Discourse* by Paul Tench. Websites include EnglishLearner.com, TalkEnglish.com, and World-English.org. Online service includes ToLearnEnglish.com. Software programs include Rosetta Stone. Other resources include Dr Seuss's children's books.

Responses of Survey 2

Survey 2 consists of ten closed-ended questions. It tests the pronunciation of the participants by asking questions about the sounds and rhyming of the words. The results are shown in the table below.

In this table, P1 stands for participant 1, P2 stands for participant 2, and so on. Similarly Q1 stands for question 1, Q2 stands for question 2, and so on. For each response, *C* stands for the correct answer and *I* stands for the incorrect answer. At the end of the table, frequencies are shown as to how many respondents answered correctly and how many gave incorrect answers.

Table 7: Survey 2 results

	Q1	Q2	Q3	Q4	Q5	Q6	Q7	Q8	Q9	Q10	Total correct
P1	C	I	I	I	C	I	C	C	I	I	4
P2	I	C	I	C	I	C	C	I	C	C	6
P3	C	I	C	I	I	I	I	I	I	I	2
P4	I	I	I	I	I	I	I	C	I	I	1
P5	I	I	I	C	I	C	C	I	I	C	4
P6	C	I	I	I	I	I	C	I	I	C	3
P7	I	I	C	I	I	I	C	I	I	I	2
P8	I	I	I	I	I	I	C	I	I	I	1
P9	C	I	I	C	I	I	I	C	I	C	4
P10	I	I	I	C	I	I	I	I	I	I	1
P11	I	I	C	I	I	I	I	I	I	I	1

	Q1	Q2	Q3	Q4	Q5	Q6	Q7	Q8	Q9	Q10	Total correct
P12	I	I	I	C	I	I	C	I	I	I	2
P13	I	I	I	C	I	I	I	I	I	C	2
P14	I	I	I	I	I	I	I	C	I	I	1
P15	I	I	I	I	I	C	C	I	I	C	3
P16	C	I	I	C	I	I	I	I	I	I	2
P17	I	I	C	C	I	I	C	C	I	I	4
P18	I	I	I	I	I	I	I	I	I	I	0
P19	I	C	C	I	I	C	C	C	C	I	6
P20	C	I	C	I	I	I	C	I	I	C	4
P21	I	I	I	I	I	I	C	I	I	I	1
P22	C	I	I	C	I	C	I	I	I	C	4
P23	C	I	I	C	C	I	C	I	I	I	4
P24	C	I	I	C	I	I	I	I	I	I	2
P25	I	I	C	I	C	I	C	I	I	C	4
P26	C	I	I	C	I	I	C	I	I	C	4
P27	I	I	I	I	I	I	C	C	I	I	2
P28	I	I	I	I	I	I	I	I	I	I	0
P29	C	I	I	I	I	I	I	I	I	I	1
P30	I	I	I	C	I	I	C	I	C	C	4

Common Pronunciation Difficulties Observed Among Native Arabic Speakers Learning to Speak English

	Q1	Q2	Q3	Q4	Q5	Q6	Q7	Q8	Q9	Q10	Total correct
P31	I	C	I	C	I	I	C	I	I	C	4
P32	I	I	I	I	I	C	C	I	I	I	2
P33	I	I	I	I	C	I	I	I	I	I	1
P34	C	I	I	I	I	I	C	C	I	C	4
P35	C	I	I	C	I	I		I	I	I	2
P36	I	I	I	I	I	I	C	I	I	I	1
P37	C	I	I	C	I	I	C	C	I	C	5
P38	I	I	I	I	I	C	C	C	I	I	3
P39	I	I	I	C	I	I	I	I	I	C	2
P40	I	I	C	I	I	I	C	C	I	C	4
P41	I	I	I	I	I	I	C	I	I	I	1
P42	I	I	I	C	I	I	I	I	I	I	1
P43	C	I	C	I	I	I	I	C	C	C	5
P44	C	I	I	C	I	I	I	I	I	I	2
P45	I	C	I	I	I	I	C	C	I	C	4
P46	C	I	C	I	I	C	I	I	I	I	3
P47	C	I	I	I	I	I	C	I	C	C	4
P48	C	I	I	C	I	I	I	C	I	I	3
P49	C	I	I	I	I	C	C	C	I	I	4

	Q1	Q2	Q3	Q4	Q5	Q6	Q7	Q8	Q9	Q10	Total correct
P50	C	C	I	I	C	C	C	I	I	C	6
Correct	21	5	10	20	5	10	29	15	5	20	Avg. 2.8
	42%	10%	20%	40%	10%	20%	58%	30%	10%	40%	28%
Incorrect	29	45	40	30	46	40	21	35	44	30	Avg. 7.2
	58%	90%	80%	60%	90%	80%	42%	70%	90%	60%	72%

Only one-fifth of the respondents got half or more of the questions right, and the average number of correct answers by respondents was 2.8 (28%). More than half (58%) of the respondents got question 7 right, where in both words *ow* is pronounced /ō/. Forty per cent or more got questions 1, 4, and 10 right. In question 1, *o* and *u* were both pronounced the same. This may be because the phonemes /o/ and /u/ are not easily distinguishable in Arabic, and therefore, the same sound is often given to both. Likewise, in question 10, *roll* and *role* were pronounced the same. However, in the case of question 4, they were able to distinguish between the sounds of /s/ and /z/, which happen to be the same as two of the phonemes of Arabic.

On the other hand, only 10% of respondents got questions 2, 5, and 9 correct. While the sounds /s/ and /z/ exist in the Arabic language, having the sound of /s/ follow a long vowel sound may have been confusing. It is more typical for /z/ to follow a long vowel sound as in *cheese*, a pattern the English learner might instinctively adopt as a general rule. In the case of question 5, distinguishing between /e/ and /a/ can be difficult for Arabic speakers, since they need only distinguish between three vowel sounds: fattah, kasra, and dumma, which could be likened to /a/, /i/, and /u/ in English. The sound /e/ may be confused with /a/ or /i/, while /o/ may be confused with /u/. In the case of question 9, the inconsistency in the sound of words with *oo* likely played a role as only five respondents got question 3 right as well. The difficulty in distinguishing between /f/ and /v/ is also evident in the poor results for question 6.

The results overall show that native Arabic speakers are not gaining much expertise in correct English pronunciation and there is a lot of room for improvement.

CHAPTER 5

CONCLUSION

Pronunciation is a correct way of speaking a word and sentence. People who speak a language from their earliest childhood naturally learn the correct pronunciation of the language. However, those who learn a language as a second language during their childhood, and especially in adulthood, face difficulties in pronouncing the words of the language correctly. The situation becomes even more difficult when their native language is significantly different than the new language. These issues are also found when native Arabic speakers are learning to speak English.

English is the third most spoken language in the world. Mandarin Chinese ranks first on the list, and Spanish is the second most spoken language in the world. The approximate number of native speakers of the English language is 335 million.[2] English is a language spoken

---

[2] Source: *Ethnologue* 2013

extensively in the realms of business and academia. Hence, it is important for non-native people to learn the language as a tool for communication and knowledge assimilation.

Pronunciation is a correct way of speaking a word. It also refers to a graphic representation of the way a word is spoken, using phonetic symbols. A native speaker is someone who has spoken a particular language since he or she were a baby, rather than having learned it as a child or adult. A native speaker of a language is someone who speaks that language as their first language rather than having learned it as a foreign language.

Arabic and English are two very different languages in terms of writing system and direction of writing. English and Arabic languages originate from two different families of languages. This is a major reason that native Arabic speakers find it difficult to learn English. The Arabic alphabet is different from the English alphabet. In the Arabic language, the adjective comes after the noun, and there is no stress on words or syllables. Punctuation rules are very flexible. Also, there is no sound elision in the Arabic language. The Arabic language is a consonant-heavy language as compared to the English language. English has much more consonant clusters for forming words than Arabic.

English pronunciation rules are often considered arbitrary and inconsistent. There are many examples in pronunciation that show that consistency is not maintained in English pronunciation. The word *cough* does not rhyme with the words *bough* and *tough*. The word *heard* rhymes with the word *bird*; however, it does not rhyme with the word *beard*. Despite these discrepancies, the English pronunciation is not without rules, and there are various rules present for assisting in the correct pronunciation of the English language.

There are various systems for writing phonetic transcriptions of English words. Amongst these, the International Phonetic Alphabet (IPA) is the most popular system. There is also an alternative transcription system made. This system was developed by Tomasz P. Szynalski and Michal Ryszard Wojcik in the 1990s. The system is known as the ASCII Phonetic Alphabet.

There are two major problems in IPA format. The first problem is that not all fonts support IPA symbols. However, there is at least one font in all modern operating systems that supports IPA symbols. Also, many applications allow font substitution, which allows borrowing of the font. The borrowed characters will not resemble the look and style of the current font, but they will be readable. However, the best results are obtained when IPA-enabled font is used. Modern operating systems have various IPA-enabled fonts. Windows XP includes Lucida Sans Unicode font. Windows Vista includes Segoe UI, Arial, Times New Roman, Tahoma, and Lucida Sans Unicode fonts. Windows 7 and 8 include Segoe UI, Cambria, Calibri, Arial, Times New Roman, Tahoma, and Lucida Sans Unicode fonts. OS X includes Lucida Grande, Arial, Times New Roman, and Tahoma fonts. Linux includes Linux Libertine, Linux Biolinum and DejaVu Sans fonts (IPA 2013).

Another problem with IPA symbols is that usually keyboard shortcuts are not available for them. There have been two solutions devised to address this issue. One solution is to use TypeIt App for Windows. Using TypeIt involves three steps. First, the TypeIt program is executed. Second, a TypeIt keyboard is selected from the drop-down list. Third, the IPA symbols are typed and the Send button is clicked. Clicking Send inserts these symbols in the document (TypeIt 2013). The second solution is to make use of the IPA website, Ipa. TypeIt.org. This website provides a keyboard for typing IPA Phonetic symbols. The written text can then be copied into the word processor in use by the writer (Szynalski 2013, p. n.d).

Certain pronunciation in the English language is very difficult to learn for native Arabic speakers. There may be several factors responsible for this phenomenon. This study identified some of those factors and presented solutions to overcome those difficulties.

These are useful guidelines and recommendations for native Arabic speakers in particular and English learners in general. It will help them to know the weaknesses in advance and apply the remedial measures to make their learning experience as result-oriented as possible. It will increase their learning curve, and they will have a sense of direction as to how pronunciation learning should be approached in the case of the English language. It will also assist organizations that send their employees for English learning courses. They will be able to identify the most appropriate courses and the best learning resources to remove the deficiencies among their staff. Finally, it will also assist organizations that plan and offer English language courses to adjust their course content to the needs of the participants.

Effective communication is a key to success in all areas of human endeavours. For any successful transaction or business operation, it is imperative that the sender be successful in communicating the message to the intended recipient. The errors in pronunciation may affect the quality of the message, and the recipient may not exactly understand the message. Hence it is extremely important to concentrate on the pronunciation and correct it so as to come as close as possible to that of the native speaker.

Recommendations

1. For the people who are not native speakers of the English language, learning phonics can assist in achieving a near-native accent of English. Phonics is a method of teaching English to beginners. In this method, each speech sound is represented with a single symbol. They are represented in a way that closely resembles how they actually sound.

2. There are many learning resources available to improve and correct the pronunciation of the English language. Book resources include *American English Pronunciation* by Donna Hope, *English Pronunciation in Use Elementary* by Jonathan Marks, *English Pronunciation in Use Advanced* by Martin Hewings, and *Transcribing the Sound of English: A Phonetics Workbook for Words and Discourse* by Paul Tench. Websites include EnglishLearner.com, TalkEnglish.com, and World-English.org. Online service includes ToLearnEnglish.com. Software programs include Rosetta Stone. Other resources include Dr Seuss's children's books.

3. To assist in correct pronunciation, the International Phonetic Alphabet (IPA) system is used. This system is used in dictionaries, course books, and *Wikipedia*. However, typing characters of this system on computer is very difficult. An

alternative to this approach is using ASCII Phonetic Alphabet system. This system uses ASCII characters for representation. These ASCII characters all can be printed on the computer. Many applications also provide shortcut keys as well for typing ASCII characters.

4. Different dialects of the English language vary in pronunciation. Some English speakers elongate vowels while speaking. Some English speakers have a nasal pronunciation to many words. These include New York state residents and Midwestern US residents. African Americans cut words short in phrases. Other speakers do not distinguish between vowel sounds. Hence *this* is pronounced the same as the word *these*. However, in the Middle East, as in most other non-English speaking countries, English language learners will be concerned largely with learning standard English, which falls in two categories, namely American English and British English. The non-native speaker will need to decide which form of standard English would best suit his needs.

5. Language learning is an ongoing process. The pronunciation mastery is also a process that would take a significant time to accomplish. Joining institutes for such learning should be a one-time activity. There are numerous free resources

available on the Net. Students must use these available resources and learn the pronunciation of the English language on a continuous basis. Also, practice makes a huge difference in this case. A good friend for whom English is a native language may prove very useful in this regard. Conversing with him on a daily basis can result in a lot of improvement in the pronunciation of the English language.

REFERENCES

Basilicato, L. (2013). "English Pronunciation Rules." eHow. p. n.d. Retrieved from <http://www.ehow.com/way_5761661_ english-pronunciation-rules.html>.

BBC (2013). "The Sounds of English." BBC "Learning English." p. n.d. Retrieved from <http://downloads.bbc.co.uk/worldservice/ learningenglish/pronunciation/pdf/sounds/sounds_chart. pdf>.

Bee, A. (2012). "How to Learn Correct English Accent & Pronunciation." eHow. p. n.d. Retrieved from <http://www. ehow.com/how_7869060_learn-correct-english-accent- pronunciation.html>.

Buleen, C. (2013). How to Improve English Pronunciation. eHow, p. n.d. Retrieved from <http://www.ehow.com/how_5106114_ improve-english-pronunciation.html>.

Ethnologue (2013). "Summary by Language Size." p. n.d. Retrieved from <http://www.ethnologue.com/statistics/size>.

Hewings, M. (2010). *English Pronunciation in Use: Advanced: Self-Study and Classroom Use.* Cambridge University Press. p. n.d. Retrieved from <http://books.google.com/books?isbn=0521693764>.

Hope, D. (2006). *American English Pronunciation: It's No Good Unless You're Understood.* Cold Wind Press. p. n.d. Retrieved from <http://books.google.com/books?isbn=1586310542>.

IPA (2013). "Recommended IPA Fonts." TypeIt. p. n.d. Retrieved from <http://ipa.typeit.org/#recommended-ipa-fonts>.

Marks, J. (2007). *English Pronunciation in Use Elementary.* Cambridge University Press. p. n.d. Retrieved from <http://books.google.com/books?isbn=0521672627>.

Mathe, E. (2013). English Learner website. p. n.d. Retrieved from <http://www.englishlearner.com>.

Miller, G. (2012). "Most Common English Errors for Arabic-Speaking People." eHow. p. n.d. Retrieved from <http://www.ehow.com/info_8460601_common-errors-arabic-speaking-people.html>.

Page, K. (2013). "English Pronunciation Activities." *eHow.* p. n.d. Retrieved from <http://www.ehow.com/list_6549039_english-pronunciation-activities.html>.

Palmer, B. C., El-Ashry, F., Leclere, J. T., and Chang, S. (2007). "Learning from Abdullah: A Case Study of an Arabic-Speaking Child in a US School." *The Reading Teacher* vol. 61, no. 1: 11. Retrieved from <http://www.pebc.org/wp-content/uploads/2010/01/Learning-from-Abdallah-Palmer1.pdf>.

Payne, L. (2013). "Phonetic Differences between English and Arabic." eHow. p. n.d. Retrieved from <http://www.ehow.co.uk/info_8274393_phonetic-differences-between-english-arabic.html>.

Perez, A. (2013). "How to Learn English Pronunciation." eHow. p. n.d. Retrieved from <http://www.ehow.com/how_7314487_learn-english-pronunciations.html>.

Rosetta Stone (2013). Rosetta Stone website. p. n.d. Retrieved from <http://www.rosettastone.com>.

Saylor, S. (2012). "Importance of English Pronunciation." eHow. p. n.d. Retrieved from <http://www.ehow.com/about_6636066_importance-english-pronunciation.html>.

Szynalski, T. P. (2013). "The ASCII Phonetic Alphabet." *Anitmoon.* p. n.d. Retrieved from <http://www.antimoon.com/how/pronunc-ascii.htm>.

TalkEnglish (2013). Talk English website. p. n.d. Retrieved from <http://www.talkenglish.com>.

Tench, P. (2011). *Transcribing the Sound of English: A Phonetics Workbook for Words and Discourse*. Cambridge University Press. p. n.d. Retrieved from <http://books.google.com/books?isbn=110700019X>.

ToLearnEnglish (2013). To Learn English website. p. n.d. Retrieved from <http://www.tolearnenglish.com>.

TypeIt (2013). TypeIt app. p. n.d. Retrieved from <http://www.typeit.org/app/?lang=ipa>.

WorldEnglish (2004). World English website. p. n.d, retrieved from <http://world-english.org>.

ABOUT THE AUTHOR

First and foremost, I am an educator, and in my twenty-five years working in this profession, I have endeavored diligently to transfer my knowledge, skills, and values to my students so as to equip them with tools that will help them achieve a life of personal fulfillment and responsible citizenry. My personal educational philosophy includes the emphasis of more time-on-task. I believe that the more time spent on quality classroom instruction, the greater is the learning that takes place within that classroom. My students' academic performance and personal well-being are important to me. I strife to keep morale high and engage my students over the course of each session. However, in being an effective teacher, I am not only required to perform well in the classroom but also to conduct myself in an exemplary manner outside the classroom.

For the past twenty-five years, I have worked in the field of education. My qualifications include a master's in TESOL with a specialty in phonology and a doctoral degree in educational leadership, as well as a TEFL Certificate (Teaching English as a Foreign Language).

Over the years, I have held various positions in schools at home and abroad. These include that of teacher/instructor in the United States and the Middle East, head of the science departments in two schools in the United States, administrator and director positions in American colleges in Egypt, in addition to working as an educational consultant for many schools in Egypt and in the sultanate of Oman. Some notable achievements have been in conducting teacher workshops and presentations, and guiding schools in the Middle East through the American accreditation process.

It is my solemn wish to contribute to the development of my institute in a substantial way, helping it to grow into one of the most reputable and sought-after higher education institutions in the region, one that turns out students who are equipped with the skills they need to successfully hold their own in the world of work. It is the ultimate honor, partnering in this most dynamic process of life.

INDEX

Lightning Source UK Ltd.
Milton Keynes UK
UKOW03f0330100517

300806UK00001B/42/P